Art of the Middle Ages

Grades K-3

Volume 3

Brenda Ellis

Start with Volume 1 and follow history in chronological order through Volumes 2-8 or start with Volume 1 and then skip to any other volume featuring the historical period of your choice.

Northglenn, Colorado
www.artisticpursuits.com

Cover art, book design, and illustrations by Brenda Ellis
Cover design and maps by Daniel Ellis
Edited by Ariel Holcomb and Daniel Stone
Student works were created in art classes taught by Mrs. Ellis from 1992-2010 and 2016.

ACKNOWLEDGMENTS

Thank you to Dover Publications Inc., New York, Art Resources, New York, and National Gallery of Art, Washington for supplying the fine art images by the great masters. Thank you to students whose work appears in the student gallery for inspiring and encouraging others through your artwork. Very special thanks go to my husband, Dan, for working with me on this project and for your invaluable thoughts, opinions, critiques, artworks, and research.

COPYRIGHT

© 2018 by Brenda Ellis. Electronic material © 2018

Manufactured in the U.S.A.

All rights reserved. No part of this book and video content may be reproduced in any form or by any electronic or mechanical means, including information storage and retrieval systems, without permission in writing from the publisher, except by a reviewer who may quote brief passages in a review. Published by Artistic Pursuits Inc., Northglenn, Colorado 80233. This book and video set is intended to be used for educational purposes only. All product names, brands, and other trademarks listed or pictured within the contents of this material remain the property of its owner and no association or endorsements between the owner and Artistic Pursuits Inc. exists. Artistic Pursuits Inc. does not manufacture art supply materials or promote sales of specific materials. The author and/or publisher is not liable for personal injuries incurred while using this book and video set or the materials chosen to go with it. Neither the author, nor the publisher can accept any legal liability.

BIBLIOGRAPHICAL NOTE

ARTistic Pursuits, Art of the Middle Ages, Grades K-3 Volume 3 is a new work, first published by Artistic Pursuits in 2018. It contains excerpts from *ARTistic Pursuits, K-3 Book One, An Introduction to the Visual Arts* © 2001, 2008, 2013.

ISBN-10: 1-939394-23-6

ISBN-13: 978-1-939394-23-1

Contents

Page   Lesson

Page	Lesson		
4		Materials	
5		Teaching Simply	
6		Welcome to the Medieval World	
7	1	Video #1 Paper Loom Weave	
9	2	People on the Move	Early Medieval
		Brooch in the Shape of a Bird	
13	3	Art in Monasteries	Medieval Illumination
		Carpet Page from Lindisfarne Gospels	
17	4	Art in Basilicas	Byzantine Mosaics
		Theotokos Mosaic	
20	5	Video #2 Panel Drawing	
21	6	Art to Instruct	Gothic Panel Painting
		Saint Francis with Scenes from his Life	
25	7	Art in Churches	Romanesque Altarpiece
		Saint Martin Sharing his Cloak	
30	8	Video #3 Stitching	
31	9	Art on Fabric	Medieval Textiles
		The Norman Fleet Lands at Pevensey	
35	10	Video #4 Straw Loom Weave	
36	11	Art in Castles	Medieval Tapestry
		The Devonshire Hunting Tapestry - Boar and Bear Hunt	
39	12	Video #5 Book Binding	
40	13	Art in the Bestiary	Book Illumination
		English Bestiary	
43	14	Video #6 Low-Relief	
45	15	Art on Book Covers	Treasure Binding
		Missal with Virgin and Child, Evangelists and Saints	
50	16	The Icon	Eastern Orthodox Iconography
		Icon of Saint George	
55	17	Art in Windows	Gothic Glass
		Chartres: Northern Rose Window	
58	18	Art on Buildings	Gothic Architecture
		The Kings, Notre Dame de Paris	
62		Objectives	
63		Bibliography	

Materials

The art materials used throughout this book are listed below. Having these items on hand will simplify the preparation for each art class. You can conveniently pull required materials from your stock as needed according to the list in each lesson. Keep in mind that items listed under STARTER PACK MATERIALS were used in volume one of this series and may already be in your stock.

ART MATERIALS

Gesso, small bottle
Gold acrylic paint, 2 oz.
Tissue paper (assorted colors)
Sculpey®, white, 2oz.
Flat watercolor brush, ½ inch
Mod Podge®, matte finish
Small tip squeeze bottle
Plastic sewing needle, large
Bristle brush, 1 inch
Lightweight chipboard*
Gold origami paper

HOUSEHOLD ITEMS

Scotch® tape
Heavy weight foil
Paper towels
Container for water
Four drinking straws
Yarn, assorted colors
¼ yard of burlap, cut 9" x 12"**

*Chipboard can be purchased or cut from cereal boxes and other lightweight food container boxes.

** Each ¼ yard of cloth will make four pieces. Two pieces are needed for each child.

STARTER PACK MATERIALS

Watercolor crayons
Oil pastel set
Scissors
Watercolor brush, *round #8*
Watercolor paper
Construction paper
Eraser
Ebony® pencil
Elmer's® Glue-All
Glue stick

Teaching Simply

We designed the ARTistic Pursuits® art curriculum to activate thought and creativity throughout every part of the lessons. In the video, your child sees how art materials are used. With the book, your child is able to internalize information that only comes through contemplation and discussion. Our combination of video and book utilizes the strengths of both formats.

ARTistic Pursuits® provides answers to the big questions of art. How do I use the art materials and what do I teach? A video lesson introduces each new art medium, providing both adults and children with the knowledge they need to handle the materials. Simply watch the video with your child, provide art materials, and then step back while your child creates an original work of art about subjects of his or her choosing. Book lessons utilize interaction between adults and children, followed by a time of working independently. Look at PREP NOTES in each book lesson for helpful hints on getting started. Read the lesson to your child. Engage in the discussion and help your child connect the narrative to his or her personal experiences. Discuss the art works by the masters, as prompted by the text. Make sure you ask the art questions in a fun, exploratory fashion. It's not a drill and there are no wrong answers. It's about gently stretching your child to see more within the picture. Your child's observation skills develop quickly and thrive with your presence and encouragement. Provide materials for the art project and your child will create an original work using his or her own ideas and experiences. We provide learning objectives to help define the overall goals of each project. See Objectives on page sixty-two. These objectives clarify good learning experiences, which helps parents to avoid expectations that are above grade level.

Each lesson is simple. It takes only ten minutes of your time, and yet your involvement is crucial to learning. It's easy. It's fun. With ARTistic Pursuits®, you *can* give your child an excellent art education.

Welcome to the Medieval World

Knights, monks, castles, and churches will all be introduced in this period following the Classical art of the Roman Empire. It is called by many names: the Middle Ages, the Dark Ages, the Medieval Period, or the Age of Faith. It's no wonder that people have trouble naming this glorious and difficult thousand years. This is an age of conflict; a long time of nation invading nation until there was little left of art, literature, or societal structure. It is remarkable that even a few men, claiming that they had understood the nature of God, built entirely new forms of communication through the earthly materials of stone, wood, and glass. Messages of hope were prevalent in the art of this age. You will encounter messages of good-deeds and courageous acts that were carried out by Roman soldiers, monks, and others who sought to bring light to a very dark world. Let's begin our journey through the Middle Ages.

-Brenda Ellis

In this period of European history, the West is centered in Rome. The East is centered in Constantinople, now called Istanbul.

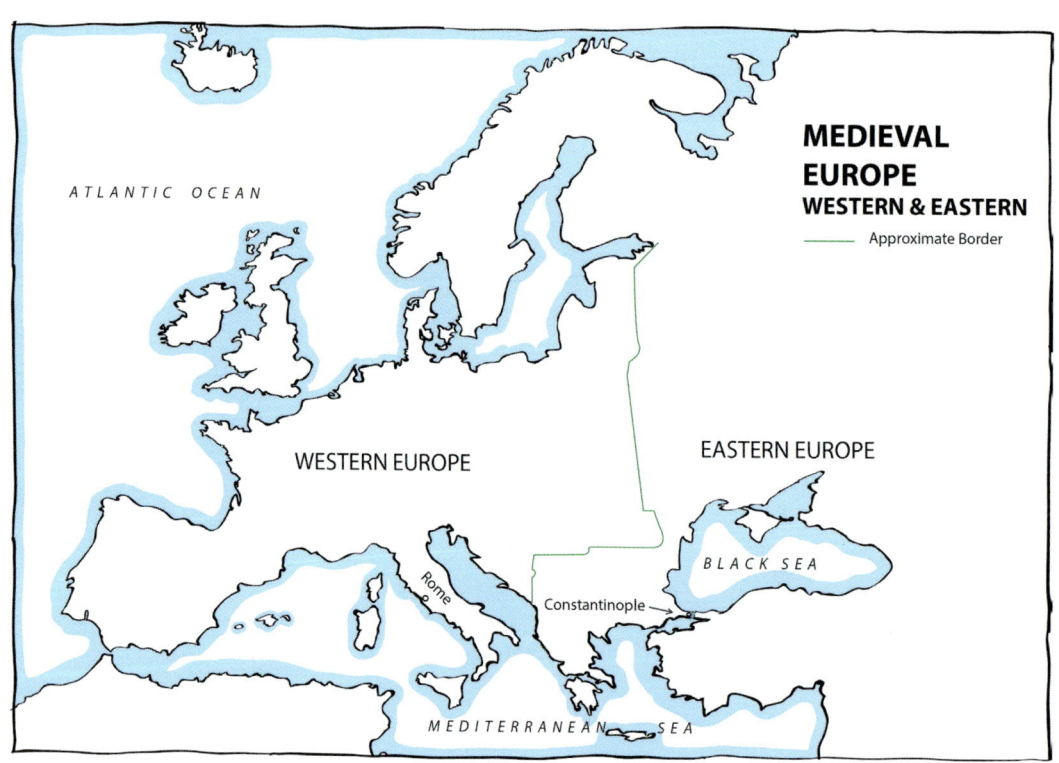

Paper Loom Weave

Lesson 1
Video #1

> Gather construction paper, gold origami paper, colored tissue paper, scissors, Elmer's® Glue-All, and a pencil.

Weave with a paper loom by following these steps.

1. View Video #1 to see how to cut, weave, and paste paper strips on a paper loom. If weaving is a new process for you, complete only the paper loom weave today.

2. Determine if you will move on to the paper crown project in the same period or at a later time. The paper crown project shows various processes for working with paper. These processes will be used in future lessons. Your art project will be unique as you apply the methods shown in the video to your own ideas.

PREP NOTES FOR LESSON 2

The paper loom weave project lays the groundwork for all types of weaving projects by introducing the over/under pattern. You may want to use the vocabulary of weaving for better communication with your child. Weaving involves strips, called **wefts**. The paper that we weave through is our **loom** and the strips on it are called **warps**.

When coloring onto construction paper, use wax crayons or watercolor crayons, but do not add water to activate the pigment in the watercolor crayons. Construction paper falls apart when wet. Work alongside children on the weaving projects until each child understands the process. Create a weaving of your own to demonstrate the steps as children make theirs with their own hands. For children, the physical act of making the motions is more helpful than just watching the process. More help will be needed for younger students, but even four and five-year-old children can successfully weave. The most common problem for children is that they tend to start the second weft in the way they started the first, either both under or both over. If this happens, show your child why this won't work by sliding the second weft strip behind the first. Oops! It's time to re-weave that second weft by starting **opposite** the first. If the first weft starts over, then the second must start under. Once it's through, slide it down to the first weft. This time it butts up against the first weft without sliding behind it. Yea! Keep your tone positive, while allowing your child to weave and make some mistakes in the process. Mistakes can be easily fixed.

OUTSIDE THE HOME ENVIRONMENT

Demonstrate one step at a time and have children repeat what you've done after each step. When instructing a group outside the home environment, set some ground rules for scissors before passing them out. Children should only cut paper and they should only hold the scissors in their hands when they cut paper. Scissors should be on the table while they watch you demonstrate the processes. By clearly demonstrating the proper use of tools, you will set up clear guidelines for future projects that will help children to have better focus and attention. It often works well to have tools and materials laid out on a table before class begins. After demonstrating the process, allow children to gather their tools and select colors of paper. In this way, they have a vision for the possible outcomes of their own project and can make better choices.

People on the Move
Lesson 2
Early Medieval

In the first half of the first millennium AD, people moved in large numbers from one place to another. This time is called the Migration Period. Roman armies moved into all of Western Europe, the Middle East, and North Africa. Rome was later invaded by the Huns from the East and the Germanic tribes from the North. Even though some art was made, it did not survive for long. Materials for art and metal work were scarce and that made them valuable. When the art was not destroyed in battle, conquering armies melted it down or took it apart to be made into something new. As the battles continued, during the Middle Ages, a new kind of art began to be made. People remembered the kinds of artworks that Romans had created in the past. They added Germanic designs passed down from their ancestors. They used these materials and designs to explain the ideas of a new faith that rose out of Judaism and the life of Jesus Christ. Three very different cultures, Romans, Germanic tribes, and Christians, had all clashed as they came together. Yet, when united in art, they produced forms that were described by the people of their time as "pictures of heaven."

Brooch in the Shape of a Bird, AD 500-600
Vendel Migration Period

Metal work was important to people on the move. Bronze helmets and weapons meant strength to those who wore them. Metals obtained in war could be melted down and reshaped on the field with fire and a hammer. A chieftain might carry a bronze dagger or fasten his cloak with a large brooch like the one above. Germanic tribes loved patterns. They wove one piece over and under another. This brooch was made of metal during the Migration Period. Look at the way the wing of the bird goes over the body and then under the tail.

The metal worker curved the bird's head so that its bill touches what other part of the bird?

Where has the metal worker used stamps to repeat a design or to make a pattern? Which pattern looks like stitching?

YOU WEAVE BEASTS

Gather construction paper in two colors, scissors, a pencil, watercolor crayons, and a glue stick.

STUDENT GALLERY
Felicity age 6

In the Middle Ages, strange creatures were painted. Their limbs and tails wove in and out of a tangled design. It is your turn to make up two strange creatures and weave them together. Select two colors of construction paper. Fold each sheet into thirds and cut on the folds to make six pieces. (1) Make three cuts into the bottom part of one piece in each color. (2) Weave the two pieces together. Glue to hold. (3) Draw and cut out heads for the creatures. Glue them to the bodies. Color the heads and bodies with crayons. Cut out tails, feet, or wings from the remaining pieces. Use your imagination just like a medieval artist.

1 2 3

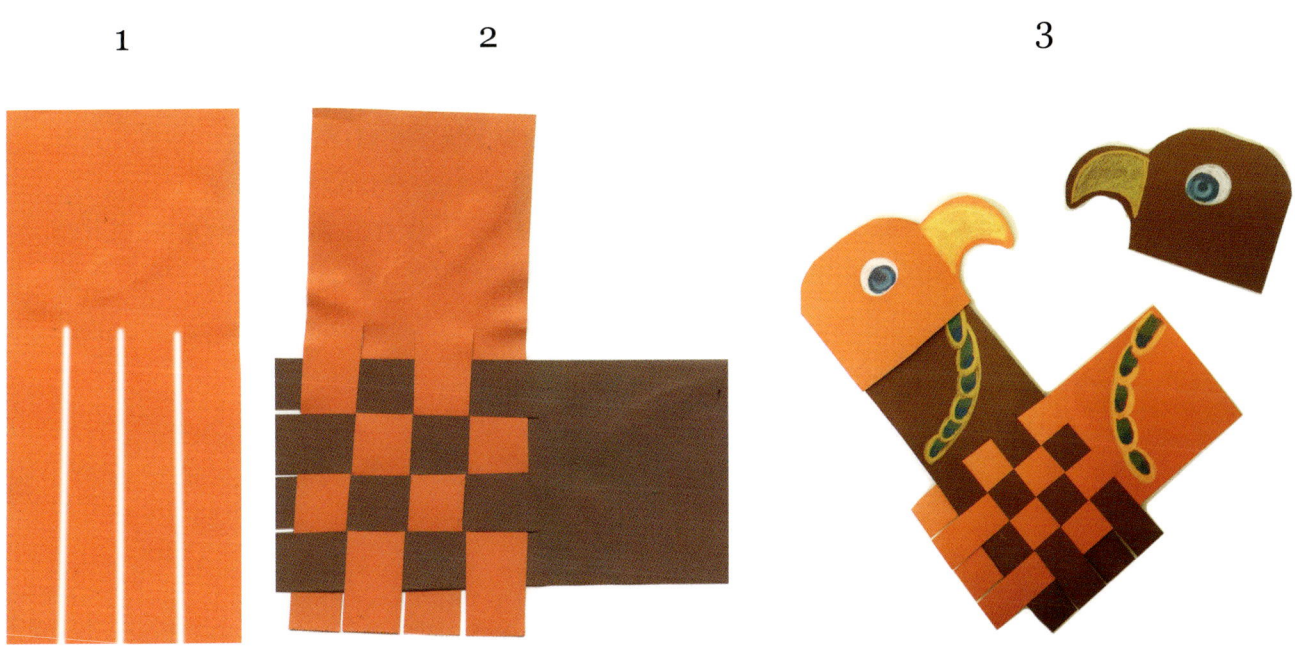

PREP NOTES FOR LESSON 3

A Pinterest search for "initials" can result in many inspiring ideas for your child. You may want to print out some ideas to share. Simple ideas are best. Those that incorporate animals and plants with the initial will best represent the goals of this project.

The first step, to draw the initial on the gold paper, will be the most challenging task in this project. You may wish to draw the initial for a young child that is not yet writing or help your child understand how to make an initial shape. Talk about what the initial looks like in lines. Then show your child what the initial looks like as a shape. You or your child might practice on a sheet of white paper. Cut out the letter from the white paper, then, flip it over as you trace around the edge and onto the back side of an origami sheet. Once the letter is drawn, your child can cut and glue the other elements of the design.

OUTSIDE THE HOME ENVIRONMENT

When instructing a group outside the home environment, think through how you will have students create their own initial. This will be determined by the ages of your group. Kindergarteners may need help. You could provide a pattern with each child's initial on it. Third graders can make the letter outline on their own. To make sure that each child gets through this part of the task easily, you may want to draw the shapes of the letters that your students will use on a large sheet, black board, or white board. Young students may need to practice on a piece of drawing paper first. Help children who have difficulty, but do not step in as long as the child is working. Do not expect perfection. Children need to do these tasks themselves in order to learn.

Art in Monasteries
Lesson 3 — Medieval Illumination

If you wanted to tell a story in the Middle Ages, you would probably speak it, rather than write it in a book. In those days, books with pictures were not common like they are today. Monks wrote books by hand. These men were protected by the walls of the monasteries that they lived in. They were trained in fancy writing, called calligraphy, and in painting pictures. The pictures are called illuminations because the gold that they used lit up the page as the light reflected from the brilliant surface. British and Irish Monks created a unique kind of art during the migration period from AD 300-900. The geometric overlapping design is an influence of the Germanic tribes. Eadfrith, who later became the Bishop of a large monastery on Iona Island, created the Lindisfarne Gospels. A portion of a page can be seen here. It is a work on vellum with colors that are taken from plant, animal, and mineral sources.

Can you find the two birds in this part of the design?

Can you find the eyes, the beaks, the dotted wings, and the tails?

Turn the page and look for more creatures. Their heads and feet lay at the ends of the colored curls!

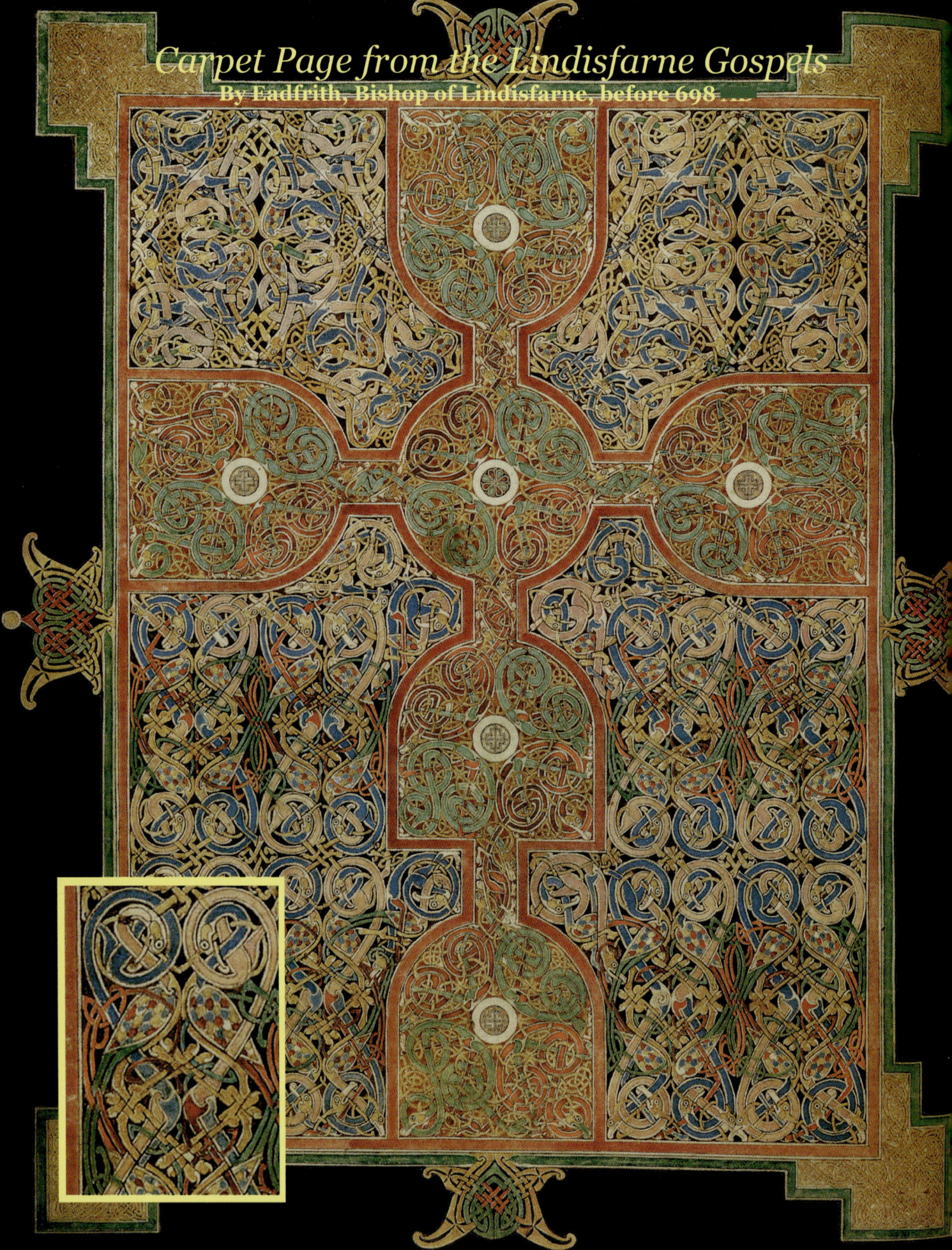

Carpet Page from the Lindisfarne Gospels
By Eadfrith, Bishop of Lindisfarne, before 698 A.D.

YOU MAKE AN INITIAL PAGE

Gather construction paper, scissors, gold origami paper, watercolor crayons, a pencil, and a glue stick.

STUDENT GALLERY
Merida age 4

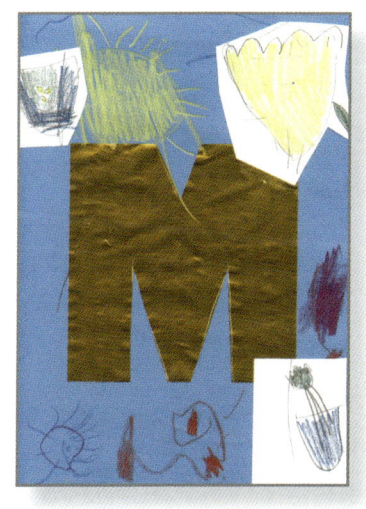

Books had carpet pages, as seen on the left, and initial pages. An initial is the first letter of a word or a name. In the Middle Ages, artists made the first initial on a page BIG. They decorated it with objects and colors. You may want to explore some initial pages, with an adult on the internet, to see how others have created beautiful pages that say something about them. Then, you make an initial page that includes some of the things you like and tells others about you.

1. Draw the shape of the first letter in your name. Draw the letter big to fill up a 6″ x 6″ gold sheet. Cut the letter out and glue it to a sheet of construction paper.

2. Draw and cut animals and other designs from colored paper. Glue the back of the designs and attach them to the full sheet. Draw details with crayons.

15

PREP NOTES FOR LESSON 4

Any kind of paper can be used for mosaics. You might want to provide textured papers, paper with patterns, prints, or magazine pages. You may want to help your child to cut the strips or provide strips in the width that you want them to work with. Paper strips can be cut with a paper cutter for a more perfect shape, if desired. Children can then snip off as many squares as needed. When large pieces are used, such as one-inch pieces, less time is required to fill the page. This size is better suited to very young children with short attention spans. If using small pieces, from one-half to three-quarter inch strips, more time is needed. Two class periods may be necessary in order for children to finish the project. This size is best suited to older children.

OUTSIDE THE HOME ENVIRONMENT

Making a mosaic takes more time than many other forms of art. For that reason, when working with groups, you may choose to cut the strips and place them in piles in the center of the table according to color. You may want to snip pieces during the class period, depending on time restraints.

Art in Basilicas
Byzantine Mosaics
Lesson 4

In the year 313 the Roman Emperor, Constantine the Great, declared that Christians were no longer criminals of Rome. With this change, Emperor Constantine had much to think about. How would this empire of people, who worshiped the many gods of Greece and Rome, become an empire that believed in one God, as the Christians did? How would people worship or show devotion? Where would they meet? He built a church based on the familiar model of Roman government buildings. The basilica was a long building. On the inside, it looked like a long open hall. Entering from one end, people moved forward toward the other end, where church officials carried out the duties of the services. Incense provided rich smells. Choirs provided sounds. And as we shall see, gold and brilliantly jeweled pictures provided the sights. The basilica model held many people and was the perfect building for the new faith.

Theotokos Mosaic, before AD 867
Constantinople, Byzantine Empire

This mosaic was added to Constantine's church, the Hagia Sophia; a church that had been without pictures for over 100 years. Imagine a world without pictures and then imagine how excited people were to see this golden, glistening imagery in the dome above them. On the day that the gold-tiled mosaic was first unveiled, a message that Jesus was both God and a man was preached by the patriarch, Pholios (Zucker and Harris). Church authorities had argued for centuries thinking that he had to be one or the other. The art showed him as both. What a surprise! The circle around the child's head represents him as God, the creator of Earth and the heavens. When the artists sat him on the lap of his mother, they represented him as a human being with a mother. The message that the church sent out to the people that day had an even greater impact because the art was a mosaic made of gold. In a mosaic, small pieces of colored glass, precious stones, and metals were arranged. Lit only by candles, the jewels and gold-covered glass glimmered and sparkled as the pieces caught the flickering light of the candles. This lighting effect gave an otherworldly appearance to the picture.

What parts of the picture look like things we have on Earth?

What parts of the picture look heavenly or unlike our normal surroundings?

YOU MAKE A MOSAIC

> Gather construction paper, gold origami paper, scissors, a pencil, and a glue stick.

STUDENT GALLERY
Linsey age 9

You just looked at a mosaic of glass and gold. Make a mosaic using colored paper. You can cut gold origami paper as well as colors to make your mosaic. Design a picture of a person.

1. On black paper, draw outlines of the objects in the picture. Draw the lines so that you can see where to put the paper pieces. Make the objects large enough so pieces of paper fit into them.

2. Cut strips of brightly colored paper. Then cut the strips into many small pieces. Use colors that you want to put into the mosaic.

3. Using a glue stick, press the glue onto one piece at a time. Press the squares of paper within the outlines on the black paper. Fill up all the spaces with bits of paper

Panel Drawing

Lesson 5
Video #2

> Gather tissue paper, Mod Podge® adhesive, a bristle brush, a container, a chipboard sheet, and watercolor crayons.

To make a panel drawing, plan two sessions. Follow these steps.

1. Select a photograph of a colorful song bird.

2. View Video #2 to see how to create a tissue paper background for your crayon drawing. Your art project will be unique as you apply the methods shown in the video to your own ideas.

Art to Instruct
Gothic Panel Painting
Lesson 6

> **PREP NOTES FOR LESSON 6**
> With your child, gather a selection of small twigs. Glue them onto a sheet of chipboard in preparation for the artwork. Plan two sessions with drying time between the sessions.

In times of safety, parents teach their children to trust their neighbors. In times of war, parents teach their children to fight, and that's what they had done for hundreds of years. How could the new Church shift the minds of the people from acting violently to being kind to their neighbors again? They could not write letters to tell people how to behave because paper, like we have today, was unknown in the Middle Ages. Most children had not been taught to read. You might think that they could simply speak messages of love and forgiveness, and they did! Church services were held throughout each day, but the people spoke different languages and many could not understand what was being said in the services. Finally, it was decided that pictures could be used to instruct others on how to behave. Paintings were made on wooden panels. Scenes were painted on each panel and then stacked together and placed in front of the altar so that everyone could see them. This altarpiece, by Masaccio, has three scenes. Some altarpieces had over twenty scenes!

Saint Francis with Scenes from his Life; by Bonaventura Berlinghieri, 1235. Church of San Francesco, Pescia, Italy.

Medieval panel paintings showed a new kind of spiritual hero. They were real human beings who lived holy lives. We call them saints. The side pictures, called apron scenes, show the good deeds performed during the life of the saint.

We know three stories that were told about Saint Francis and birds. One story tells of how he asked a boy to release a cage full of birds that were about to be sold for someone's dinner. Another story tells of him preaching in one language to a large crowd that spoke many different languages. He stretched out his arms where a number of birds landed and as he preached, they interpreted the message, each bird to each unique language so that everyone heard his words. This scene tells of Saint Francis's sermon to the birds. We see Saint Francis with two other monks. The birds on a hill face him as they listen to his words. The message of this scene is about telling the good news to every creature, no matter how small and insignificant they are. He tells the birds, "With every beat of your wing and every note of your song, praise Him" (Fox Ellis). The Franciscans followed this way of thinking and built churches on the edges of cities, where the poorest lived, so that they could help those with the deepest needs.

Look for clues, in the portrait on the previous page, to identify which of these three figures is Saint Francis.

Do the birds respond to the message by turning towards Saint Francis or by flying away?

Do Romanesque buildings appear on all of the apron scenes or on only this scene of the birds?

The background color of the painting is a symbol of heavenly light. What color is it?

YOU MAKE A PANEL RELIEF

Gather a chipboard sheet, twigs, Elmer's® Glue-All, tissue paper cut into 4″ x 4″ pieces, construction paper, Mod Podge®, scissors, a container, and a bristle brush.

STUDENT GALLERY
Angelica age 9

You just looked at an outdoor scene of Saint Francis with trees and birds. He tells the birds the good news of his faith. Think of a scene where you could tell a creature some good news. It might be an animal, bird, or a person.

1. Gather small twigs. Use white glue to attach the sticks to a chipboard panel. Let it dry completely.

2. Pour about 1/4 cup of Mod Podge® into a container. Brush over the sticks with Mod Podge®. Attach small pieces of tissue paper in brown or the color of your choice. Brush over the top of the tissue paper.

3. Brush Mod Podge® onto the area around the tree. Apply the tissue pieces. Some objects can be cut from construction paper. The snowman and his hat, above, was cut from construction paper and applied on top of the tissue paper. Brush Mod Podge® over the top of the completed picture. When finished, rinse the brush with mild soap and warm water. Set the picture in the open air to dry.

24

Art in Churches
Romanesque Altarpiece
Lesson 7

> **PREP NOTES FOR LESSON 7**
> Before beginning the project, discuss the types of good deeds that your family values. Share stories of your good deeds with your children. Help your children remember good deeds that they have done. In a classroom setting, simply give an example and allow a few children to share. Discussion will help children to generate ideas for their art.

The church was a big part of a person's life in the Middle Ages. At a time when there were few freedoms, the church was the one place that everyone could enter – from the poorest peasants to the wealthiest lords and kings. People came and went to services throughout the day. Those living far away made pilgrimages to large churches in Rome and Canterbury. They came to receive forgiveness or to seek miraculous cures for their illnesses. In the early Middle Ages, massive *Romanesque churches* were built in ways that still kept the Roman building style of the basilica. This type of church was designed to be a journey from the time people entered the doors to the time that they exited, with many attractions along the way. Religious relics were displayed in circular side rooms, like a museum today displays articles of interest. Artwork painted on wood panels lined the walls and covered the front altars. To the medieval visitor, these attractions were mysterious, colorful proofs that heaven had come to earth.

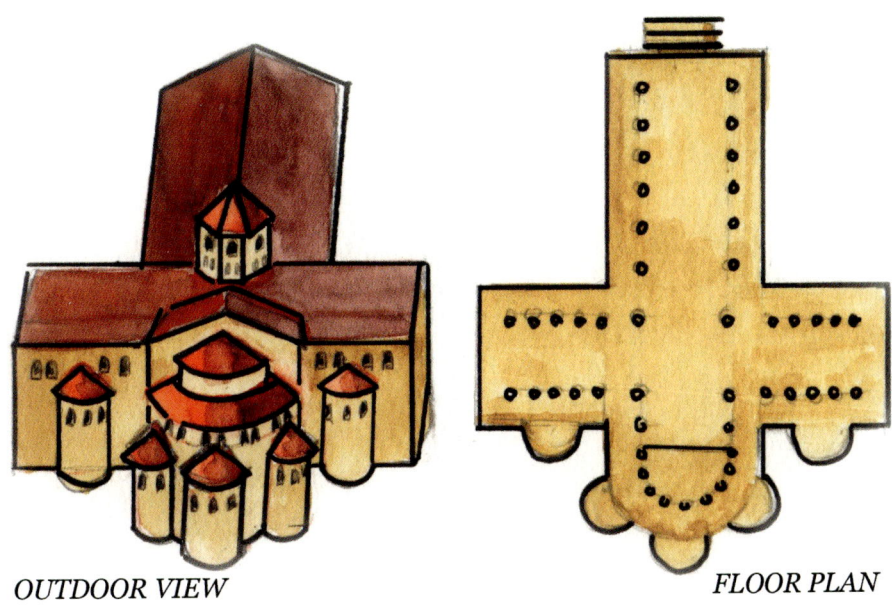

OUTDOOR VIEW   *FLOOR PLAN*

Detail of Saint Martin Sharing his Cloak. *Christ in Majesty,* Altar Frontal from St. Martin de Puigbo', 12th Century, the Vic workshops. Ancient town of Vic in Catalonia, Spain

This section of the *Christ in Majesty* altar stood at the front of the church for everyone to see. The scene shows the kind act of a Roman soldier called Martin of Tours. His story places him in Gaul, riding into the city on his fine horse with sandaled feet, a helmet, shield, armor, and a woolen cloak. Roman soldiers were powerful. When Martin raised his sword above the head of a poorly clothed, starved man, people feared that the old man was in trouble. But Martin did something unusual. Seeing that the man had no coat to keep himself warm, Martin swung his sword and cut his own cloak in half. He gave one part to the man and kept the other for himself. This type of kindness was unheard of by a Roman soldier, but Martin had heard Christian teachings and he understood its values of feeling for the needs of others and giving when one could do so. The news of Martin's act of kindness spread quickly so that many heard that this Roman soldier had shown compassion and charity. People said he was a hero. When Martin's service in the Roman army was finished, he became a Monk and started new churches all over the country of Gaul. In this painting of Saint Martin, bold black outlines surround the figures. Black lines stand out from the gold background. The bold colors in the art meant that everyone who entered the church would see the charity of Saint Martin.

Can you name the bold colors used by the artist?

Where is the horse's head?

Where is the red cloak that was cut in half?

How does the artist show that the man is poor? (You might look for the following: torn clothing, showing the rib bones and other bones, eyes droop downward in sadness.)

YOU MAKE A COLLAGE

Gather construction paper, a scissors, a pencil, and a glue stick.

STUDENT GALLERY
Anthony age 10

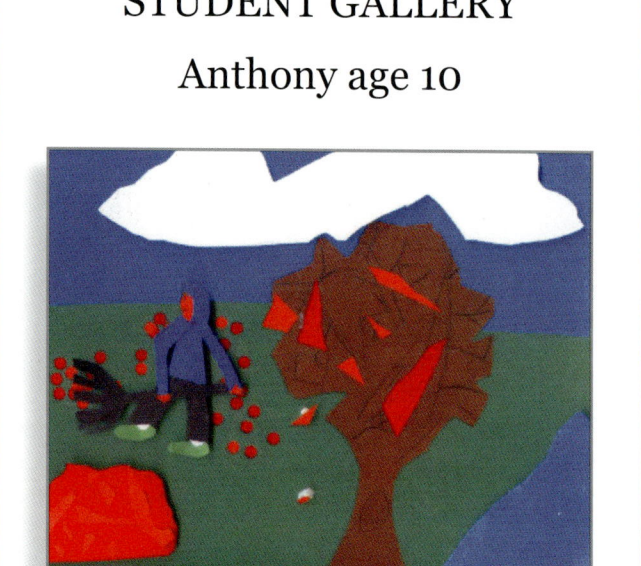

When you have compassion on someone who needs help and you decide to help that person, you are doing a good deed. Taking action to help others is a value that has been passed down from the early days of Christianity to our culture today. In the STUDENT GALLERY, we see a picture of the day that Anthony helped his parents rake leaves in the yard. You have stories of good deeds too. Tell your story in a collage picture.

1. Draw shapes of objects on colored paper. Draw over the lines with a black watercolor crayon to make the figures stand out.

2. Cut out each piece. Glue the pieces together to make the whole figure.

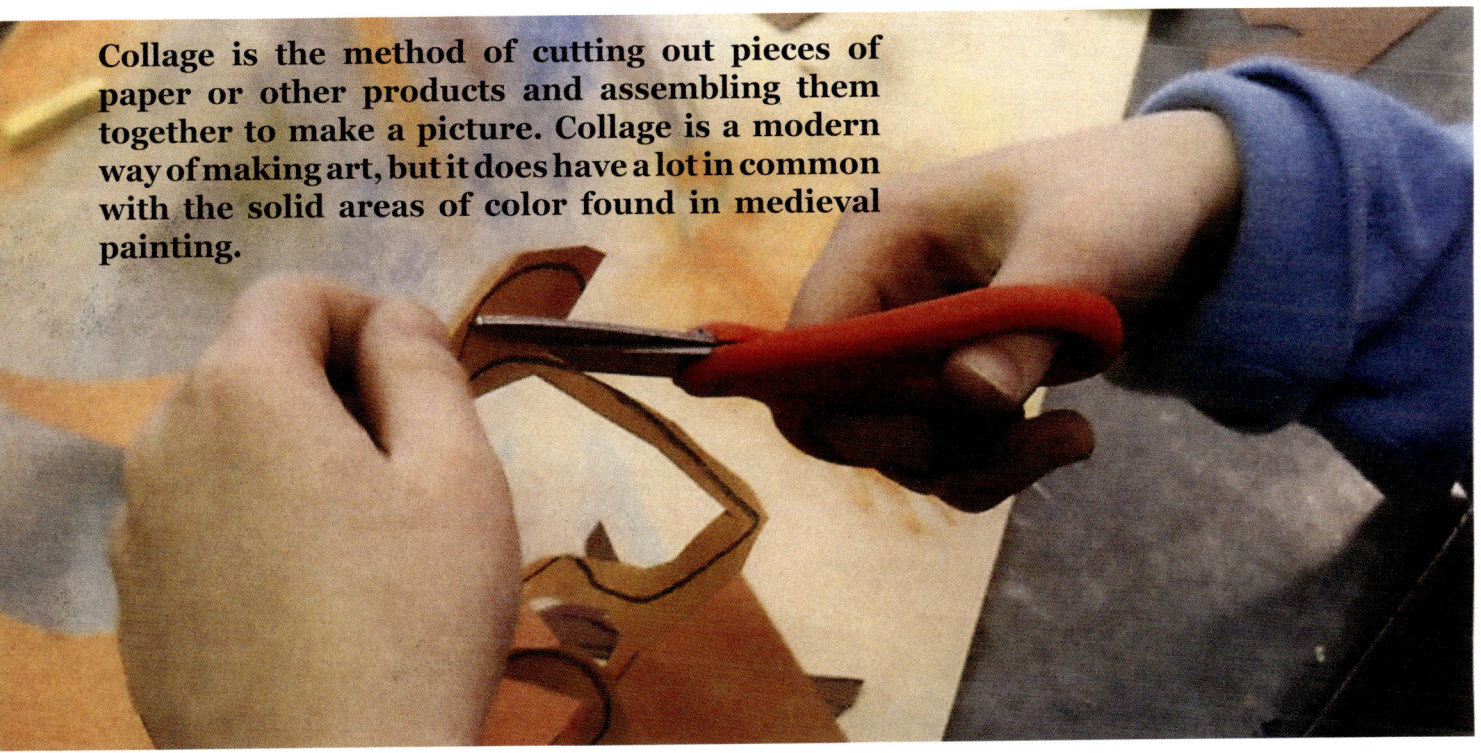

Collage is the method of cutting out pieces of paper or other products and assembling them together to make a picture. Collage is a modern way of making art, but it does have a lot in common with the solid areas of color found in medieval painting.

3. Draw black lines to show details such as the bark on this tree. Draw outlines around figures such as the bird.

4. Glue all the pieces to the paper to make a colorful collage that tells your story.

Stitching

Lesson 8
Video #3

> Gather burlap fabric, chipboard, scissors, pencil, plastic needle, yarn of various colors, tape, and glue.

To make art with stitches, you will need drying time after preparing a chipboard frame. Follow these steps.

1. Select an object for your art. You might choose an animal or a person dressed in medieval clothing.

2. View Video #3 to see how to make a picture using stitches. Your art project will be unique as you apply the methods shown in the video to your own ideas.

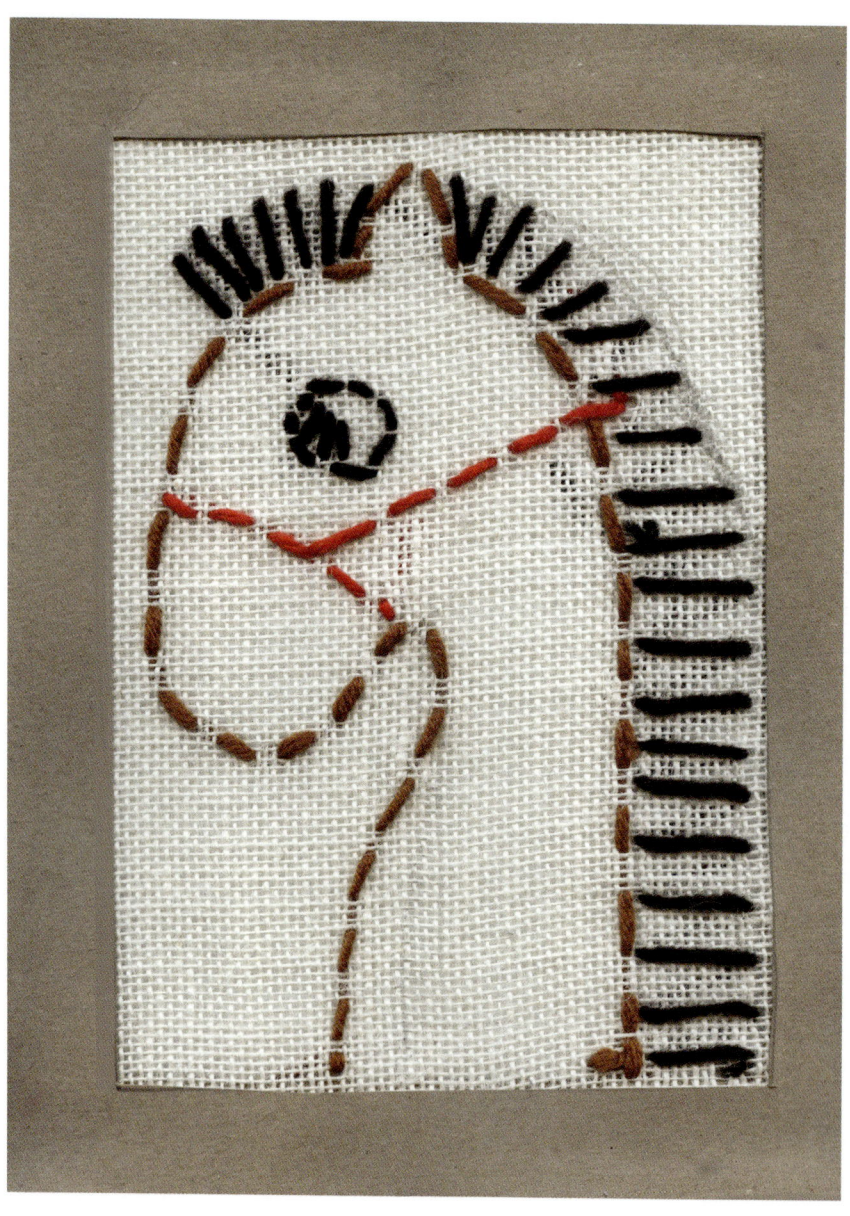

Art on Fabric
Medieval Textiles
Lesson 9

PREP NOTES FOR LESSON 9

You and your child might enjoy watching The Animated Bayeux Tapestry-You Tube. Always preview it first. You can stop at "William prepares for Battle" if you don't want to view the battle scenes. *www.youtube.com/watch?v=LtGoBZ4D4_E*

Before beginning this project, you or your child must prepare a chipboard frame as shown in Video #3. Allow the frame to dry completely. Heat setting locks the color into the fabric and prevents smearing. Use an iron to heat set the oil pastel picture once it is finished. Place the picture color side up on a safe surface. Place a sheet of copy paper on top. Set the iron at medium heat. When hot, move the iron over the paper for one or two minutes. Allow the frame to cool.

Life in the Middle Ages lacked a lot of things that we have today. Wealthy people had horses. Those who did not, walked everywhere that they wanted to go. Homes had little furniture, no books, and possibly a single cup that was used by the whole family. In this environment, fabric was highly valued. People typically owned one set of plain clothing. At this time, people with wealth began decorating cloth by sewing stitches into it that made pictures. A medieval person's reaction to a piece of decorated fabric was one of complete awe. They saw signs of wealth. A cloak with a black lion on a red background spoke to them of their ruler. When they looked upon red robes and gold embroidered sashes, they saw symbols of those that had spiritual power. Cloth was so rare that in Northern Europe it was used for money, to buy other objects. Men might cut a chunk of cloth out of their bag to use as payment for cattle.

The Norman Fleet Lands at Pevensey, 1066
Canterbury, England

From start to finish, it was women who oversaw all textile work. Embroidery, like you see here, was the most costly way of decorating cloth in the medieval period. Imagine women, protected by castle walls, sewing a record of history. The Bayeux Tapestry is an embroidered cloth that stretches to nearly the length of a football field. Into this huge length of fabric is stitched the events that happened from 1065 to 1066 when the Normans traveled in boats to make war with England. The center strip shows the action of the story. A lower strip shows creatures encountered on the journey, both real and imagined. This huge cloth was the treasured item of a conquering King.

What animals do you see in the lower strip of this section? What animals are imagined? What animals are real?

What animals do you see in the top strip? Can you see birds?

What are some of the activities of the men in the boats? Do they travel with horses?

Where are the men who have mounted their horses and ride off to battle? Can you see their mail armour, swords, and shields?

YOU STITCH

> Gather oil pastels, burlap fabric, chipboard frame, scissors, glue, yarn, and a plastic needle.

Make a picture that tells of a past event in your life. Have you taken a trip, moved into a new home, or celebrated a birthday? The picture can tell the story so that the event can be remembered. Use oil pastels and stitching.

STUDENT GALLERY
Antoine age 9

Color a picture onto the burlap fabric with oil pastels. An adult will set the color with an iron.

Thread the needle. Tie a knot in the back of the picture.

Sew a straight stitch around the frame. Push the needle up near the frame's edge and loop the yarn around the frame.

34

Straw Loom Weave

Lesson 10
Video #4

Gather yarn in two colors, four large straws, and Scotch® tape.

To make a weaving, follow these steps.

1. Select one color of yarn for the warp threads and another color for the weft threads.

2. View Video #4 to see how to make a weaving with yarn. Your art project will be unique as you apply the methods shown in the video to your own ideas.

Art in Castles
Medieval Tapestry
Lesson 11

PREP NOTES FOR LESSON 11
Help your child to find a picture of an animal to use as a reference for an animal painting.

A large tapestry had a practical purpose. Like a heavy rug, hung high on the wall over open spaces, it could block the cold winds of winter or the heat of the summer sun. Tapestries also added color to the colorless interiors of these buildings made of stone and wood. Designed by artists, the scenes were meant to be admired and enjoyed. An elaborate tapestry, like the one below, might very well have been the focus of entertainment for a day with one's guests.

The Devonshire Hunting Tapestry- Boar and Bear Hunt, 1425-35 Flemish, Southern Netherlands

This tapestry features a hunting party and is purposefully complicated in its design. It is very large. Gentlemen, ladies, dogs, and the creatures that they hunt are all brought together in what looks like a tangle of activity. This causes our eyes to leap from one subject to another and must have kept party guests entertained for hours as they looked at the piece. The wild game obtained during a hunt was an important source of food for people at this time. Hunts were followed by feasts where meat was cooked and preserved. The hunt became a social event for European nobility, making it a perfect theme for a large tapestry.

Can you find some dogs which are used for the hunt? What kinds of wild animals are hunted? What are the most interesting hats or clothing items that you see? What color do the trees and plants introduce into the picture? Can you find castles in the background?

YOU MAKE AN OUTDOOR PICTURE

> Gather construction paper, scissors, a pencil, watercolor paper, watercolor crayons, a container, a brush, a paper towel, and a glue stick.

You just looked at a medieval tapestry featuring a hunt. The theme of a hunt gave the artist opportunity to draw and paint a variety of costumes, animals, and plant life. Find a photograph of an animal that you want to draw. Cut a sheet of watercolor paper down by one inch on all sides.

(1) Draw a picture of the animal in an outdoor scene using watercolor crayons. Allow the painting to dry. Apply glue to the back of the picture and adhere it to a sheet of construction paper. (2) With a scissors, snip from the outside edges of the construction paper to the watercolor paper. Weave yarn and paper strips around the edges and glue the pieces to complete your tapestry.

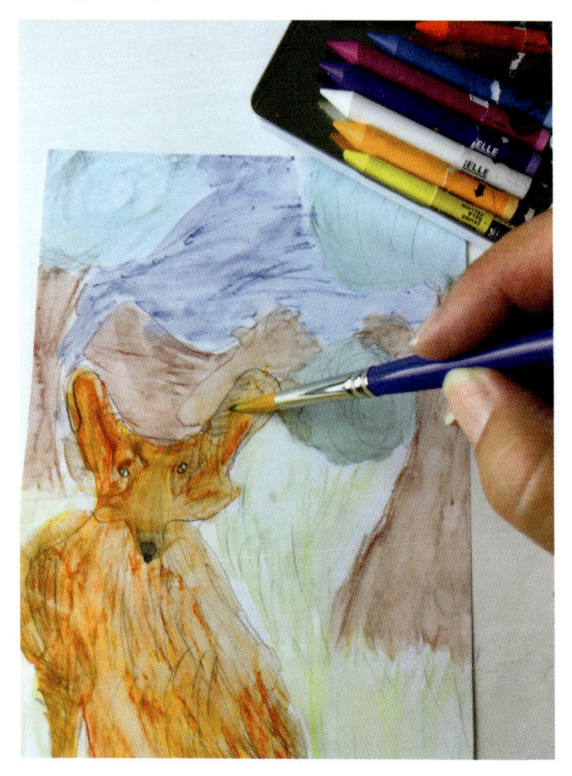

STUDENT GALLERY
Cassandra age 8

Book Binding

Lesson 12
Video #5

Gather watercolor paper or sketch paper, watercolor crayons, water container, a brush, a paper towel, a pencil, construction paper, yarn or string, Elmer's® Glue-All, and a paper punch.

To illustrate and bind a book you will need several sessions. Follow these steps.

1. Think of a story idea. Follow the instructions for creating the four parts of a story.

2. View Video #5 to see how to make story pages and a cover for your story and stitch it together with a book binding stitch. Your art project will be unique as you apply the methods shown in the video to your own ideas.

See page forty-four for additional suggestions for groups.

39

Art in the Bestiary
Book Illumination
Lesson 13

> **PREP NOTES FOR LESSON 13**
> Secretly, find a picture of an animal to use as a descriptive reference for your child's animal painting. Have fun with your child! There is no right way or wrong way to draw the verbal description. When only one verbal description is given to a group, children can see what different things their imaginations bring to their works.

A type of book, called the Bestiary, was popular in the 12th and 13th centuries in England and France. This book shows beasts such as animals and birds. Many illustrations for the Bestiary were drawn by artists who had never seen the real animal. They used verbal descriptions, which were provided by people who had seen the animal, as guides to their drawings. Then they imagined what the animal looked like. The words in a Bestiary described the animal and told moral stories based on the animal's natural behaviors. Pictures like this one were copied in other manuscript illustrations and possibly used for guides in stone carving, wall painting, and stained glass.

Have you ever seen a real lion? Have you seen a photograph of one? Does this picture of a lioness with her cubs look like a real lioness? What parts look like a lion? What parts do not look like a lion?

English Bestiary, 13th Century
North Midlands, England

Look at an illuminated page from an English Bestiary. The page is split into three scenes. This page is a story read from top to bottom. The top scene shows a male lion. **What does the lion see on his journey?**

A lioness is shown in the middle scene.

How many cubs do you see in the middle scene?

What do you think the red area represents? Could it be a cave or grassy nest that makes up her lair?

Both male and female lions are featured in the bottom scene. **How many cubs do you see?**

Can you tell which cubs are boys and which are girls by matching the colors to the colors of the parents?

Have the cubs left the lair and entered the world that their father roamed through in the top scene?

41

YOU MAKE A BESTIARY PICTURE

> Gather drawing paper, watercolor crayons, and a photograph of an animal that you don't see, but another person selects.

You just looked at an illumination from a book about animals. The artist probably had never seen this type of animal. Find out how easy or difficult it is to draw from a verbal description. Another person will choose an animal from an image in a book. Do not look at or know what kind of animal it is. The other person will describe the animal in detail. Draw a picture of the animal using just the words you are told about the animal. Have fun with your picture.

STUDENT GALLERY

Tamsen age 6

Low-Relief

Lesson 14
Video #6

Gather a sheet of chipboard, Elmer's® Glue-All, a pencil, gesso, a ½ inch flat brush, and watercolor crayons.

To make a low-relief with glue, follow these steps.

1. Select a picture of an animal that you want to use for a shield design. You may want to do a study of different types of designs for shields of the medieval period.

2. View Video #6 to see how to make a low relief picture. Your art project will be unique as you apply the methods shown in the video to your own ideas. You can refer to this demonstration for review anytime a project uses lines that stand away from the surface.

PREP NOTES FOR LESSON 15

This project is an excellent opportunity for your child to write and illustrate an original book. The entire book will take three sessions. In session one, you and your child will make a softcover book as shown in Video #5, Lesson 12. In session two, your child will design the front and back hardcovers and allow glue lines to dry in a relief. Your child can also create jewels to add to the front cover and let them dry. In session three, you and your child will attach the softcover book to the hardcover.

PREPARATION FOR SESSION ONE

Cut and prepare pages for a 9 x 9-inch softcover book. You will need the materials listed in Lesson 12. Your child may write a story or leave the pages blank, to be filled in later. Use more pages if desired. Tell your child to write on the inside pages only. The outside portion of the book will become part of the hardcover. Give your child the time needed to make this book a treasure!

When instructing a group outside the home environment, you will need a faster method of punching holes into the softcover portion of the book. You can make a cardboard template. Create a piece of chipboard that is 9 inches in length and a few inches wide. On it, draw marks where you want the holes. Clamp it onto the sheets of paper with two binder clips. Use an electric drill to make holes through multiple thicknesses of paper. One chipboard template can be used for the books of the entire group.

PREPARATION FOR SESSION TWO

Each child will need two sheets of chipboard cut 9 inches in length by 8 ½ inches wide for the hardcovers. The 9-inch side is the length of the book. Make sure that this side runs up and down as children draw the cover illustration. 8 ½ inches refers to the width of the book.

To make tissue paper-covered jewels, form flat bottomed "pebbles" with Sculpey® clay. Roll the clay on a plastic or metal surface. Unbaked clay may damage wood finishes. Bake the clay according to package directions. Cover the cooled pieces with Mod Podge® using a brush. Wrap the clay jewel in tissue paper. Drape the tissue paper over the top and tuck the edges under the flat side. Cover with another coat of Mod Podge® and allow your jewels to dry.

PREPARATION FOR SESSION THREE

Each child will need one strip of construction paper or cover paper, 9 inches in length by 2 ¼ inches wide for the spine of the book, one sheet of heavy foil cut 12 inches in length by 24 inches wide, and one back cover/front cover template as shown on page 47. The important measurement here is the 1 ¼ inch space between the back right side and the front left side. The height should be 9 inches so that the cardboard covers, made in session two, fit into the spaces on each side of the spine.

Art on Book Covers

Lesson 15
Treasure Binding

In the early part of the Middle Ages, we use the word "church" to describe a group of people who believed the message taught by Jesus Christ. During the Middle Ages, the church grew to be a large organization of people who ran governments and controlled the religious life of the people throughout Europe. The many monks who devoted their lives to the church and its message, kept learning alive for ten centuries within the church, while most people could not read or write. Monks copied scriptures and ancient writings letter by letter. It took a monk a full year to copy one Bible. They worked in a monastery scriptorium where each book was made by hand from its vellum pages to its metal jewel-laden covers. The monks did the work that you are practicing now. They learned to read new words, improved their handwriting, and practiced their art. This system would change in 1450, when Johannes Gutenberg figured out how to make copies of a book with a machine and moveable type. With the invention of the printing press, many books could be made at one time. It would be the beginning of a new period, but that's a story for another time.

Missal with Virgin and Child, Evangelists and Saints, Front Cover, 1200-1232.

Luxurious book covers using gold or silver, jewels, and ivory carvings were called treasure bindings. The metal art was attached to wooden boards with tacks. You can see the tacks in this example. Treasure bindings were made for grand illuminated manuscripts. These sat at the altar as centerpieces for church services. Like other medieval art, a center figure is surrounded by other scenes. The four gospel writers sit in each corner, with saints between them.

How many jewels are attached to the figure of the Virgin that sits in the center?

How many jewels are used in the outer edge of the book cover?

What colors of jewels do you like best?

YOU MAKE A TREASURE BOUND BOOK

> Gather chipboard pieces, scissors, glue, construction paper, yarn, brush, water container, Mod Podge®, Sculpey® clay, and tissue paper.

You just looked at a treasure binding from the medieval period. You can make a treasure binding for a book. If you don't have a current story in mind, you can bind blank pages that can be filled in later.

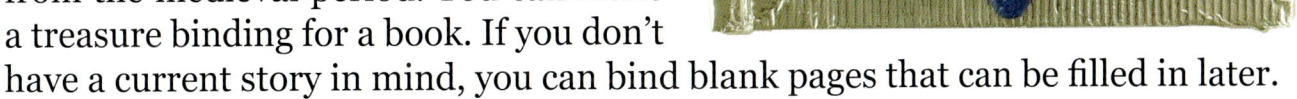

1. In the first session prepare a softcover book. Write on the inside pages only. Set it aside.

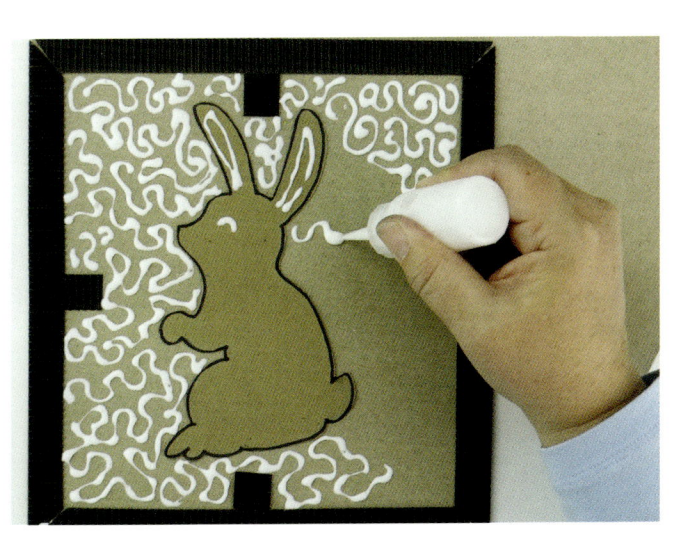

2. In the second session, use the low relief method, with glue, to make the front and back cover design. Draw a design for the front and back covers of the book on two sheets of chipboard; 9 inches high and 8 1/2 inches wide. Cover the lines with glue to make a relief. Allow the glue to dry.

3. In the third session, prepare a template as shown, 9 inches in height with a 1 ¼ inch center. This is a template to help with placing the book pieces together. You will line up the hard covers to the spine using this template.

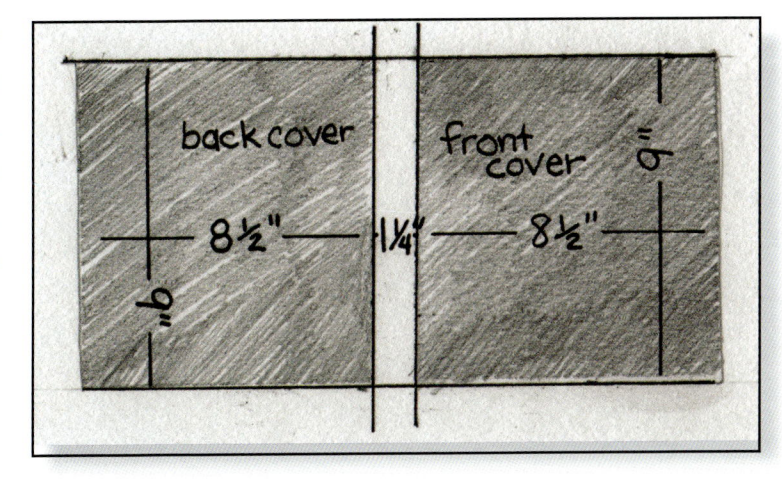

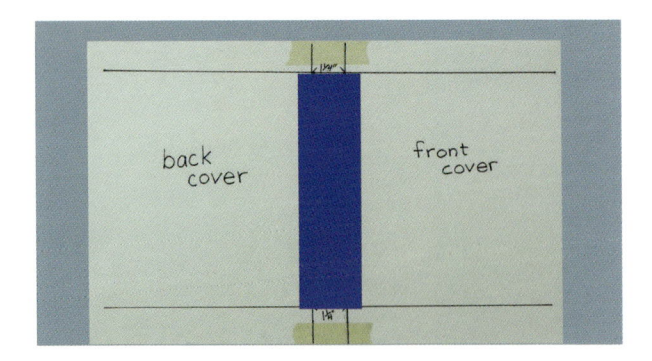

4. Cut the spine from a sheet of heavy paper to 2 ¼ inches wide by 9 inches tall. Center the spine in the middle of the template.

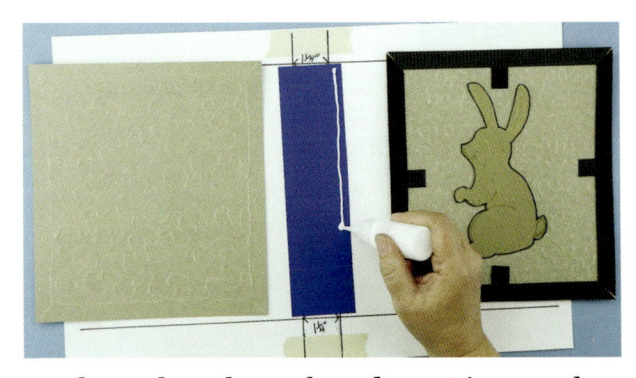

5. Place glue along the edges. Line up the front and back hard covers to the lines on the template; place them on the glued edge of the spine.

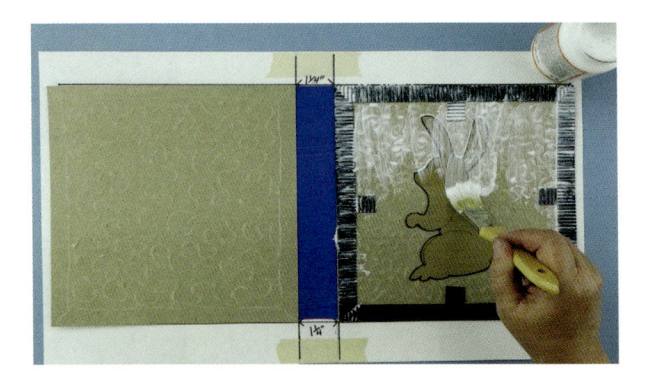

6. With all pieces securely in place, apply a layer of Mod Podge® to the front cover (right side) with a bristle brush.

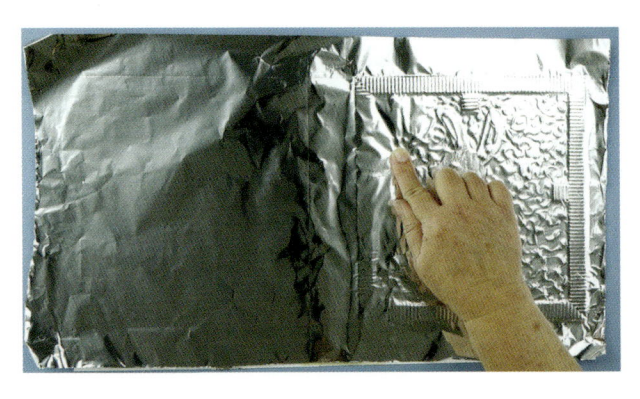

7. Place foil over the front cover that you have layered with Mod Podge®. Press your hand or fingers over the surface and watch as the foil picks up the raised lines.

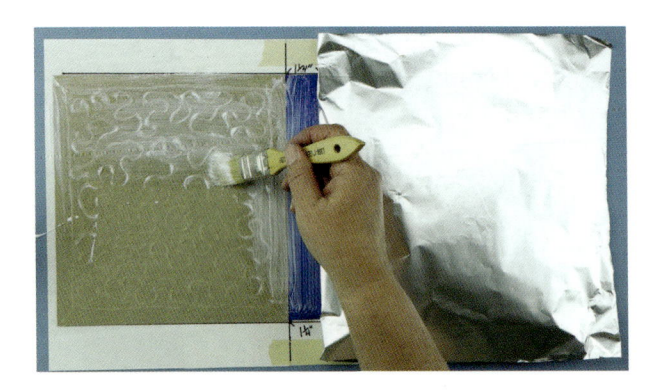

8. Fold the left side of the foil over. Apply a layer of Mod Podge® to the back cover with a bristle brush.

9. Lay the foil over the surface. Press your fingers gently over the surface of the foil to pick up the raised lines.

48

10. Flip the entire cover over to see the inside. Apply Mod Podge® to the top inch; brush all the way across the front cover, the spine, and the back cover.

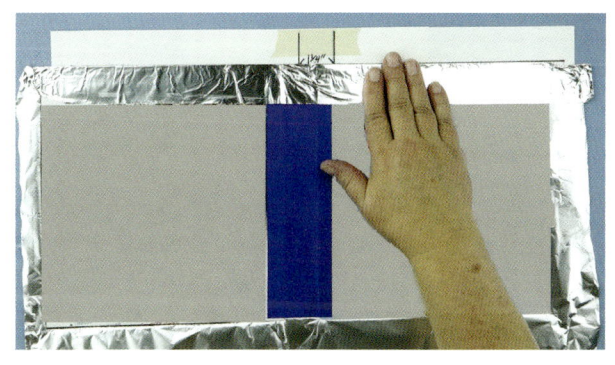

11. Fold the foil down onto the Mod Podge®. Press down. Repeat the application and fold the remaining three sides.

12. Apply Mod Podge® to the inside of the front cover (left side). Cover the foil and the cardboard.

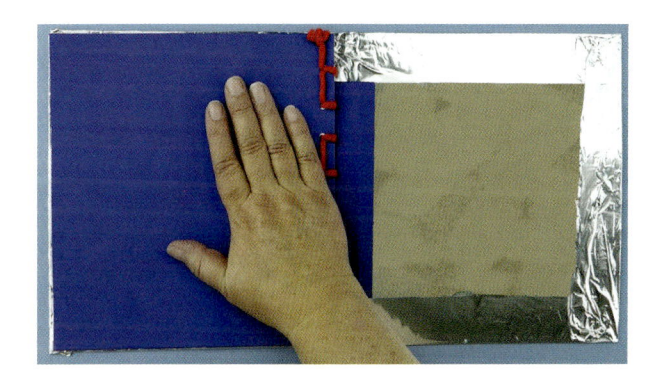

13. Line up the softcover book with the left edge, the top, and the bottom of the hard cover. Press firmly.

14. Apply Mod Podge® to the inside of the back cover (right side). Cover the foil and the cardboard.

15. Fold the book and line up the right edges. Press firmly. To prevent warping, lay heavy books on top of your book and dry overnight. When dry, glue jewels to the cover to make a treasure binding.

49

The Icon — Eastern Orthodox Iconography

Lesson 16

> **PREP NOTES FOR LESSON 16**
> Plan three sessions and allow for drying times after each session.

In the Byzantine Empire, some authorities wanted art in the church because it could remind people of the characters of the Bible. Others did not want art in the church because people might worship the objects, rather than the God they represented. In the year 754, the iconoclasts won the argument and took all traces of art out of the church. Upon seeing their precious art smashed and burned, those that liked art only wanted it more. At this time, there was little or no art within homes. There were no TVs, computers, or phones with pictures. What they did have to look on was the beauty of a flower or the colors of an orange sunset. They wondered why they should look at empty stone walls as they honor the creator of a colorful world. Shouldn't colors be inside the walls of the church? In about a hundred years, when enough people had become convinced of this idea, they made new art for the churches. They painted pictures called icons. An icon is an illustration of a story or of an event.

Icons contain elements that reminded the medieval person of how the spiritual world interacts with mankind. Let's look at how the objects in this picture tell the story of Archippus.

A church was built on a river where a healing had happened. People came often to the same spot to receive healing. Can you find the church building and the river that ran beside it?

Archippus worked at the church constantly and began preaching a salvation message to those who came for healing. Can you find Archippus at the church?

His preaching made some people mad. In an effort to destroy the church and Archippus, they diverted a second river into the first, in hopes of flooding the church and Archippus, who would not leave it. Can you find the second river that flows into the river by the church?

Archangel Michael performs the miracle and sends the raging water into a rocky cliff that diverts the water from the church. Can you find the angel and the stone that stopped the water?

Icon of Saint George, mid-1300
Lod, Israel, Eastern Mediterranean

An icon is a special type of picture. To be called an icon, the subject must be a religious one and the meaning behind the subject must be true to the beliefs of the Eastern Orthodox Church. It is to be used as a focus for prayer and thinking about the ideas of the Christian faith. This icon was made at the time of the Crusades, when Islamic nations threatened, and eventually took over the center of the Eastern Church in Constantinople. According to legend, a young Christian was captured on the island of Lesbos. The boy was forced into slavery. While the boy handed a glass to his captor, he was suddenly swept up and rescued by St. George and returned to his home. In the picture, Saint George is shown with his arm around the boy, who still holds a glass of liquid.

Do you see the boy clutching at the side of St. George?

Does Saint George wear the armor of a knight?

What do Saint George and the boy ride upon?

YOU MAKE A RAISED PICTURE

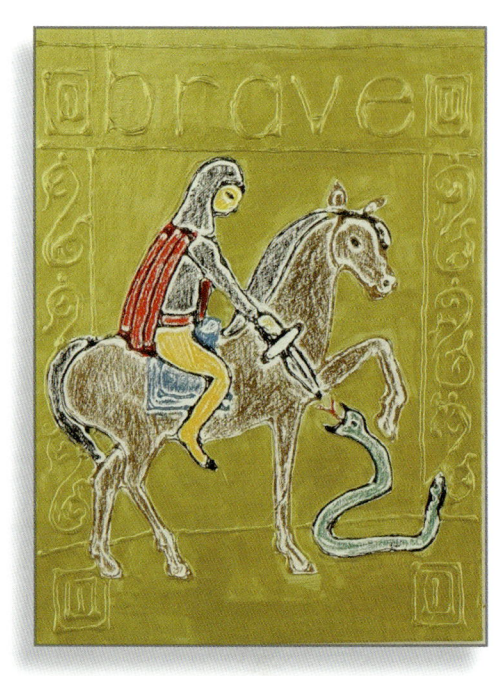

Gather watercolor crayons, gold acrylic paint, gesso, Elmer's® Glue-All, a squeeze bottle for glue, chipboard, a brush, a water container, and paper towels.

Knights had a code of chivalry which laid out some moral habits of right and wrong. These codes were sung by street minstrels, written in poems, and added to by numerous medieval authors. One code said that the medieval knight must "fight for the welfare of all." Another code said he must "speak truth at all times." And yet another was simply a word, to show "diligence." You can make a work of art that illustrates a chivalrous word. Choose a good act like "generous," "helpful," or "brave."

1. Draw a simple picture of someone acting on the word that you've chosen. Write the word on your picture.

2. Draw around the picture with glue, gently squeezing it over the lines. Wait for the glue to dry.

3. Paint over the entire picture with gesso. Allow the gesso to dry completely.

4. With crayons, draw into the spaces of the figures with color. Draw on the glue lines to make the outline stand out.

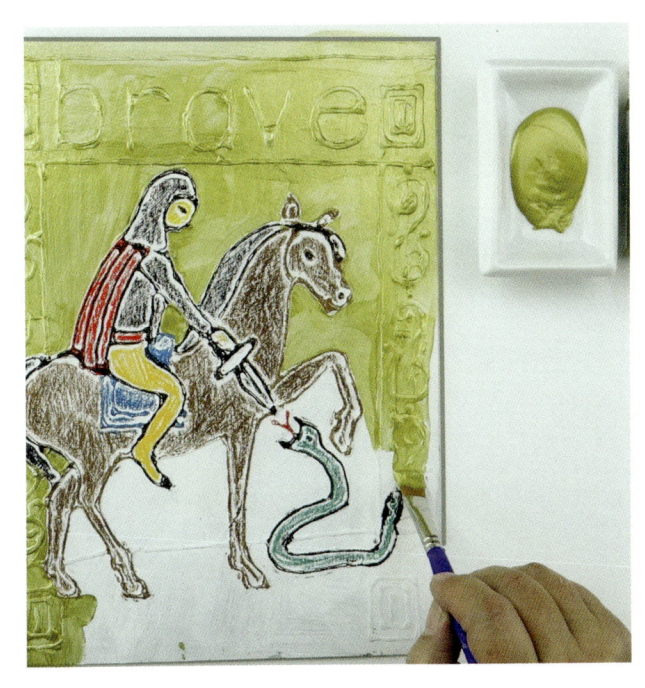

5. Paint gold over the spaces that are left uncolored. Paint carefully around the colored areas.

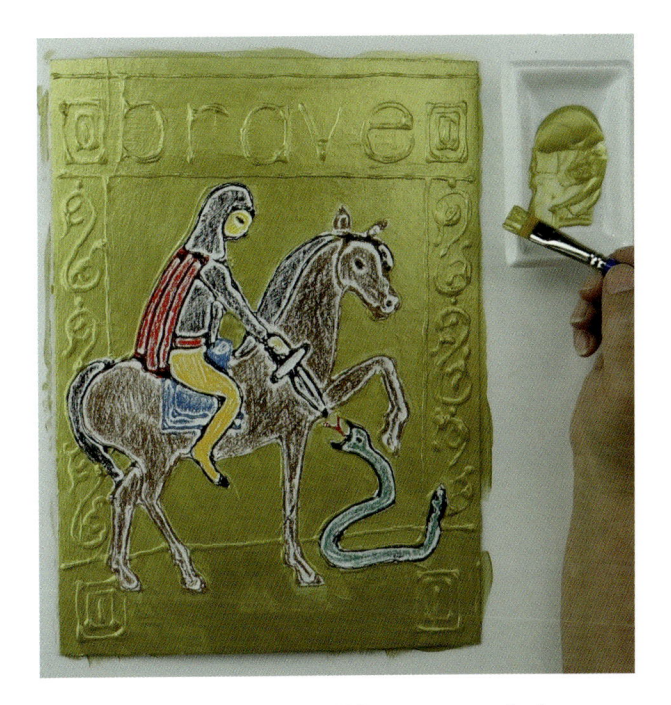

6. Paint over the gold a second time to thicken the coat of paint and make it shine!

53

PREP NOTES FOR LESSON 17

You will need to prepare sheets of various colors of tissue paper in about 4" x 4" pieces. Your child can trim the colors to the sizes needed.

As you work with your child use the terms "on the fold" and "on the edges" to describe where to make the cuts. Cuts made on the fold will create spaces within the center of the paper. Cuts made on the edges will make spaces on the edges of the paper.

OUTSIDE THE HOME ENVIRONMENT

When instructing a group outside the home environment, you will need to prepare sheets of various colors of tissue paper in about 4" x 4" inch pieces for each child. No other special preparations are needed. Children should have their own scissors and glue sticks.

Art in Windows Gothic Glass — Lesson 17

Castles, knights on horseback, peasants, kings, and great church cathedrals were all a part of living in the Middle Ages. These people had never seen a TV or movie screen where colorful images are projected with light. When they looked at stained-glass windows, it was like viewing an image of heaven as sunlight streamed through bits of colored glass. Sparkling streams of colored light flooded into the dark churches. To make stained-glass windows, glassmakers mixed clean sand with ashes from burnt wood. They melted the mixture over a hot fire. Metals were added to the glass, turning the hot mixture into brilliant colors. They scooped up a ball of liquid glass on the end of a hollow pipe, like a straw, and blew into it until a bubble formed. By quickly swirling the pipe, the bubble would flatten into a large circle. After it cooled, glasscutters cut the circle of hardened glass into shapes. The shapes were put together to make a picture using a grozing iron to shape and trim the glass. The glass pieces were held together with strips of black lead (Macaulay).

Chartres: Northern Rose Window
13th Century France

It may be hard to imagine making art with sunlight but that is what people did almost one thousand years ago. Abbot Suger (pronounced Soo-Jay) dreamed of a church building that reminded people of God as they entered it. The new church had tall pointed towers like fire to remind people that God was warmth. Light was let in through huge windows and reminded people that God was light. Large circular patterns, called rose windows, spread outwards, like the petals of a flower. The narrow windows below the rose window, are lancet windows; named because of their resemblance to a lance or spear tip.

It is recorded that people stood for hours staring at the windows. One abbot mourned the fact that he would rather stand a day in the presence of the light than a day studying the scriptures. The Christian faith was told in these pictures. It was a bright storybook that everyone could read.

Can you point to the group of windows, that when put together, make up the shape of a flower? How many lancet windows do you see in this window grouping? Can you see a figure in each lancet window?

YOU MAKE COLORED WINDOWS

Gather construction paper, tissue paper, scissors, a pencil, and a glue stick.

Make a stained glass window using colorful tissue paper for the glass and black paper to hold the work together. When the art is taped to a window, the light shines through the tissue paper just like colored glass!

STUDENT GALLERY

Callista age 7

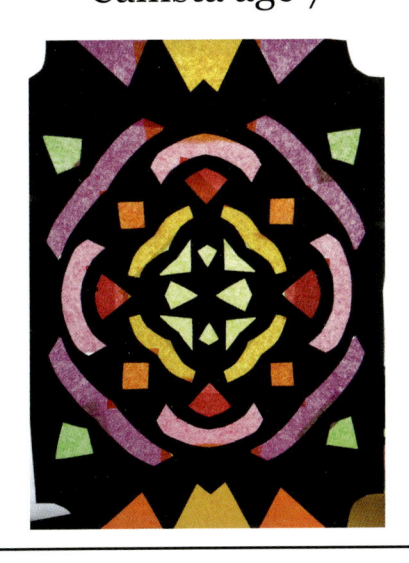

1. Fold a piece of paper in half. Fold the piece in half again. You have the option to fold one more time, bringing the two folded sides together, but this added fold sometimes makes it difficult cut.

2. Cut shapes through all layers. Cut on the two folded sides to make shapes on the inside of the final piece. Cut shapes on the open sides to make shapes on the outside edges of the final piece. Carefully unfold the black paper.

3. Cut pieces of tissue paper large enough to fit over each cut-out shape. Glue around each cut shape on the backside of the black paper. Press the tissue paper onto the glued edges. Fill each cut shape with colorful tissue paper. When finished, turn it over and hang it in a window.

Art on Buildings
Gothic Architecture
Lesson 18

> **PREP NOTES FOR LESSON 18**
> Gather the necessary chipboard pieces. Be prepared to help young children to construct the sides of the alcove. Help only as needed while allowing each child to do as much of the project as they are capable of doing. The project will require two sessions with drying times.

Abbot Suger did more than design beautiful stained glass windows. He changed the appearance of the entire building! His ideas began while studying the scriptures. Suger read that God was light and that light had come to earth. Light must be a part of the experience of the church, he thought. He said, "The dull mind rises to truth through that which is material." He meant that what we see is not a distraction away from God, as many leaders at the time thought, but can be used to transport people into a more real experience with God. To get light into the church, he would need to replace the stone with glass. His problem was that the weight of the stone in the round Romanesque arches, used for windows, pushed outward to the sides. It needed the support of heavy stone walls to hold the stones in place. When Suger designed the pointed arch, he directed the weight downward. The heavy support walls were removed and the arch rested on thin pillars. Once less stone was needed, windows replaced stone. Stone could be carved into, because less stone was needed for support. This began a tradition of elaborate stone carvings where there had once been solid stone.

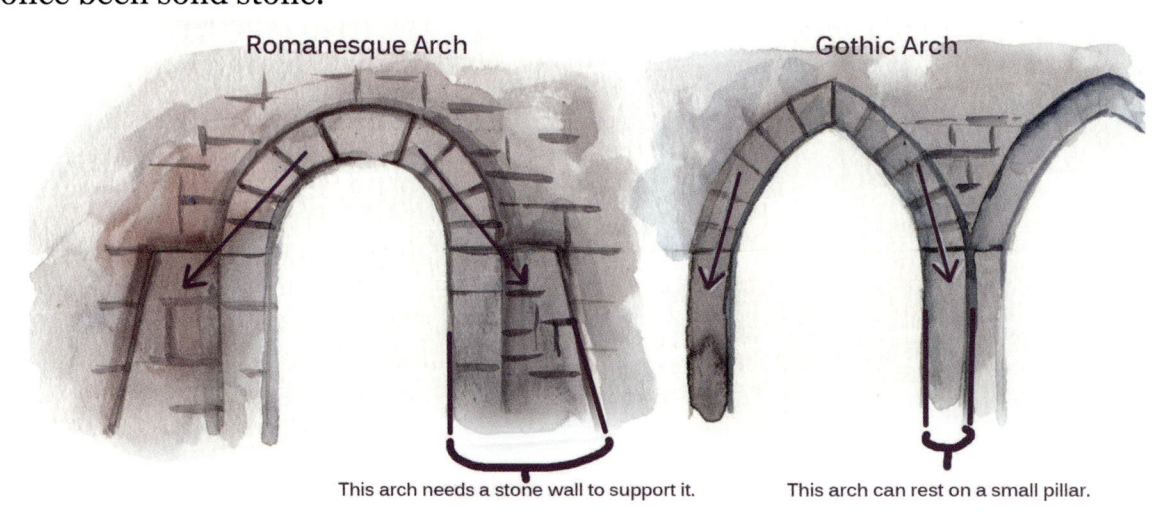

Romanesque Arch — This arch needs a stone wall to support it.

Gothic Arch — This arch can rest on a small pillar.

The Kings. Notre Dame de Paris, 1163-1345
Paris, France

The Gothic building can be recognized by more windows and elaborate carvings on the exterior walls. Carved spires rose to the sky. Figures were carved in places that had once been solid blocks of stone. The Kings of Judah are carved into niches on the West façade of the Notre Dame Cathedral. It was ordered to be built by a bishop in the 12th century and work was completed after nearly two hundred years. Imagine working on a project that you would never see completed in your lifetime. The carvings are elaborate and detailed. Rows of decorative elements line each arch. On every edge a pattern was carved.

Can you see a portion of a rose window in this picture?

Can you see lancet windows in this picture?

Figures stand between carved pillars. Are the figures all the same or is each one carved in a different way to represent a different person?

YOU MAKE A STATUE

Gather identical food boxes of lightweight chipboard, scissors, masking tape, marker or pen, two 4" cardboard tubes, glue, gesso, ½" flat brush, watercolor crayons, gold paint, and a water container.

You can see that the figures sit in alcoves on the face of the church. Draw either a Romanesque arch or a Gothic arch to put your figure into.

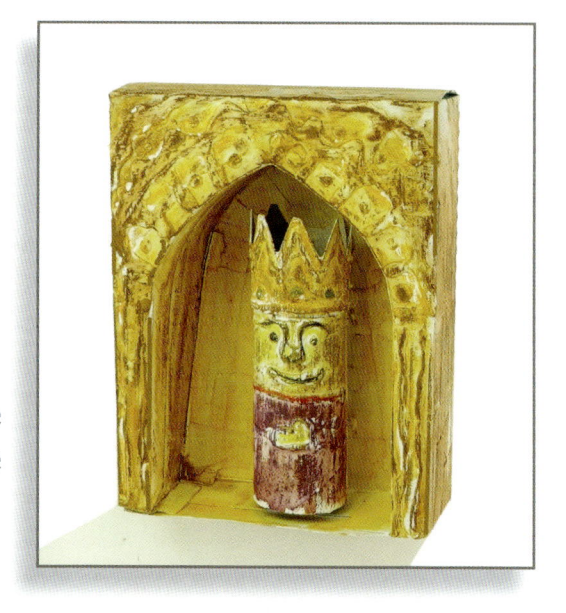

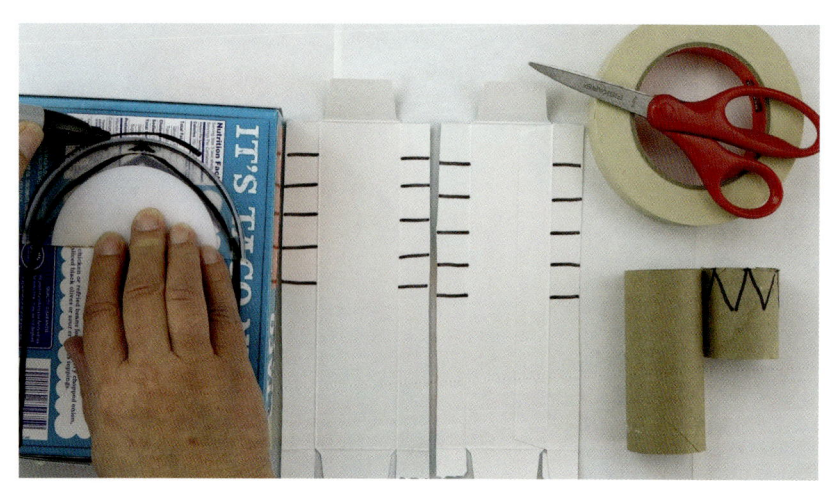

1. On the front face of one box, draw and cut out an arch. You might use a lid to draw a circle at the top of the arch. You might make a Gothic arch with a point.

On the second box, remove both sides by cutting, on the front face and back, 1/2 inch from the folds. You will leave a flap connected to each side of the two side panels. Do not cut along the folds.

2. Make slits on the flaps, cutting from the edge to the fold.

3. Join the two side pieces on one end with tape. Place the joint in the center of the arch. The slit cardboard will bend inward on the back of the box. The slit cardboard will bend outward on the front face of the box. Tape the slit cardboard in place. This is the alcove. You will place the figure inside the alcove.

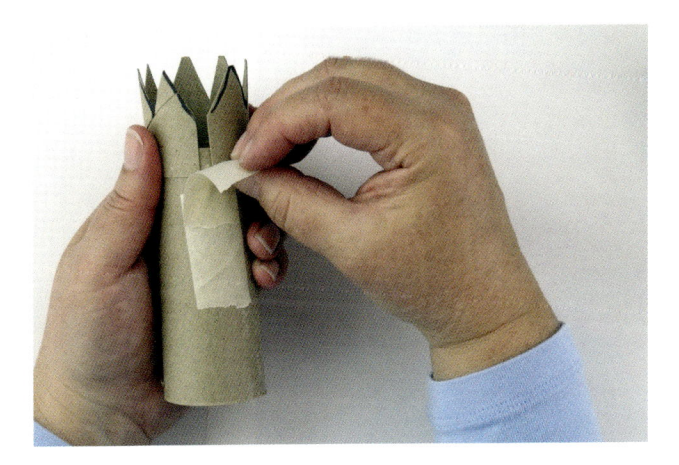

4. Cut one tube in half so that you have a two-inch tube. Cut one end of the two-inch tube to make a crown. Cut the two-inch tube lengthwise and separate it so that it can be wrapped around a four-inch tube. Attach the pieces together with tape. Attach the figure to the alcove with glue.

5. Use glue to draw the face of the king or other figure. Decorate the crown and clothing. Decorate the arch with glue lines as well. Allow all the glue to dry.

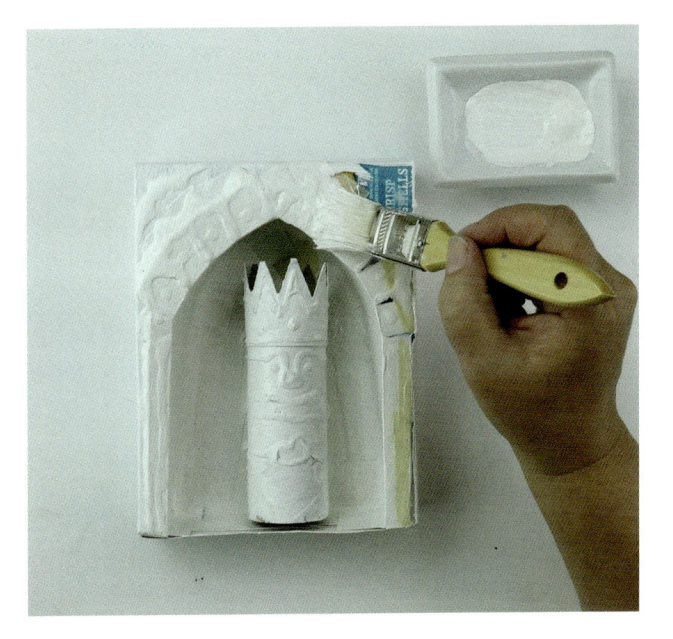

6. Cover the entire figure and the alcove with gesso. Once the gesso is dry, paint it with a final coat in the color of your choice. You can make it look like a stone structure or paint it in bright colors.

OBJECTIVES

The purpose of objectives is not to inhibit or restrain creativity in any way, but to ensure that the activity is focused clearly enough that both student and teacher know what is to be learned in the lesson. When objectives are met, your child is learning, without regard to the skill level or outcome of the art being produced.

Lesson 1: The student will be able to use a scissors to make cutouts by folding the paper. The student will be able to weave paper in an under/over pattern.

Lesson 2: The student will demonstrate his or her ability to weave paper, cut paper to make shapes, and glue paper to make an original artwork featuring two animal heads woven together to create their own Germanic-type of design.

Lesson 3: The student will demonstrate his or her abilities in drawing the shape of the initial in their first name, and then illustrate their ideas about themselves or their interests. The student may use both imaginative and realistic imagery and decoration as they draw, cut, and paste.

Lesson 4: The student will create a mosaic from pieces of paper and demonstrate his or her ability to select and assemble colors to make an image of a person.

Lesson 5: The student will illustrate a bird while demonstrating the use of outline and filling in spaces with color using crayons on a tissue paper covered panel.

Lesson 6: The student will imagine a moment when they tell good news to someone else. The panel relief method will be used to show descriptive elements through objects, colors, or symbols that describe the event.

Lesson 7: The student will create a paper collage while demonstrating his or her ability to draw, cut, arrange, and glue shapes to make a whole picture.

Lesson 8: The student will demonstrate the use of the running stitch, the straight stitch, and tying a beginning and ending knot while using yarn and a needle on burlap.

Lesson 9: The student will describe a past event in the world or in their own lives and make a work of art with oil pastels and stitching.

Lesson 10: The student will produce a sample of weaving with yarn using a straw loom.

Lesson 11: The student will make a watercolor painting and weave a border using paper and yarn.

Lesson 12: The student will demonstrate his or her knowledge of the four parts of a story while creating an original story on paper. The student creates front and back cover pages and stitches them together with the book pages using the book binding stitch.

Lesson 13: The student will draw a picture of an animal from a verbal description by another person. The artwork may or may not fully represent the physical appearance of the animal that was described.

Lesson 14: The student will use methods of low-relief in a shield design that demonstrates understanding of the terms *field* and *charge*.

Lesson 15: The student will make a softcover book with a book binding stitch and then assemble it into a hardcover treasure bound book.

Lesson 16: The student will select one word that describes a good act and then illustrate its meaning through a picture.

Lesson 17: The student will fold, cut openings on the folds and edges, and paste tissue paper over the openings to make a mock stained glass window.

Lesson 18: The student will demonstrate the use of tabs and low relief in a three-dimensional alcove with figure inside a Romanesque or Gothic arch using glue, cardboard, and paint.

BIBLIOGRAPHY

"Fox" Ellis, Brian, www.saintfrancisgarden.com. 2008. Traditional stories based on the medieval books "Fioretti" or "The Little Flowers of Saint Francis". Retrieved June 20, 2016.

Macaulay, David, *Cathedral, The Story of Its Construction,* The Trumpet Club, 1973.

MacLeish, "Chartres: Legacy from the Age of Faith", National Geographic Society, December 1969.

Setton, Ph. D., Litt. D., Kenneth M., "900 Years Ago: The Norman Conquest", National Geographic Society, August 1966.

Dr. Steven Zucker and Dr. Beth Harris, "*Theotokos Mosaic,* Hagia Sophia, Istanbul," in *Smarthistory,* December 15, 2015, accessed July 13, 2016, http://smarthistory.org/theotokos-mosaic-hagia-sophia-istanbul/.

FINE ART CREDITS

The author and publisher thank the following institutions for permission to reproduce the master works in this book.

Page 10; *Brooch in shape of Bird*, 500-600. Vendel, Migration Period. Leaded brass with a silvered surface, Overall: 2 1/8 x 1 1/4 x 3/8 in. (5.4 x 3.2 x 1 cm). Purchase, Leon Levy and Shelby White Gift, Rogers Fund and funds from various donors, 1991 (1991.308). Photo Credit: Image copyright © The Metropolitan Museum of Art. Image source: Art Resource, NY

Page 14; *Carpet Page from Lindisfarne Gospels*, before A.D. 698 by Eadfrith, Bishop of Lindisfarne. Photo Credit: Dover Publications, Inc.

Page 18; *Theotokos Mosaic*. Virgin and Child enthroned. Gold and glass mosaic. Byzantine, ninth century, before 867. Photo Credit: © Vanni Archive/ Art Resource, NY

Page 21: *The Madonna and child with Saints;* by Masaccio; 1422. Photo Credit: Dover Publications, Inc.

Pages 22,23; *Saint Francis Scenes from his Life*, 1235 by Bonaventura Berlinghieri, Church of San Francesco, Pescia, Italy, Photo Credit: Dover Publications, Inc.

Page 27; *Altar frontal from St. Martin de Puigbo' - detail of St. Martin sharing his cloak*, 12th CE. Romanesque art. Tempera on wood, 97 x 123 x 6 cm. Photo Credit: Scala / Art Resource, NY.

Page 32, 33; *The Norman Fleet lands at Pevensey*, Sept. 26-27, 1066. Detail from the Bayeux Tapestry. Photo Credit: Erich Lessing / Art Resource, NY.

Page 36, 37; *The Devonshire Hunting Tapestry - Boar & Bear Hunt*. Full view. Woven wool with natural dyes. Southern Netherlands, 1425-35. Photo Credit: V&A Images, London / Art Resource, NY

Page 40, 41; *English Bestiary*, artist unknown, 13th Century. North Midlands, England. Photo Credit: Dover Publications, Inc.

Page 46; Original front cover of a *Missal with Virgin and Child, Evangelists and Saints*. Silver gilt and jeweled plaque. Germany (Abbey of Weingarten), c.1200-1232. MS. M.710, front cover. Photo Credit: The Morgan Library and Museum / Art Resource, NY

Page 50; *The Miracle of the Archangel Michael at Chonae*. Photo Credit: Dover Publications, Inc.

Page 51; *Icon of St George,* from Lod, Israel, mid 13th CE. Egg tempera and gold leaf over a prepared pine panel, 18.8 x 26.8 cm. Photo Credit: © The Trustees of the British Museum / Art Resource, NY.

Page 56; *Chartres: Rose Window Stained Glass* The Northern rose window at Chartres: Glorification of the Virgin, with the coat of arms of France and Castile and figures from the Old Testament. Stained glass window. Cathedral, Chartres, France
Photo Credit: Alfredo Dagli Orti / Art Resource, NY

Page 58; *Rouen Cathedral at Dawn*, 1894 by Claude Monet. Photo Credit: Dover Publications, Inc.

Page 59; *The Kings, West Façade, Notre Dame de Paris*. The Kings. Gallery, composed of 28 statues representing the Kings of Judah, West facade, Notre Dame de Paris, Gothic cathedral built 1163 - 1345, ordered by bishop Maurice de Sully, d. 1196, Ile de la Cit?, Paris, France. Photo Credit: Manuel Cohen / Art Resource, NY